MW00911667

Bizarre Beast Battles

RED-TAILED HAWK VS. BURMESE PYTHON

Gareth Stevens
PUBLISHING

By Theresa Morlock

Please visit our website, www.garethstevens.com. For a free color catalog of all our high-quality books, call toll free 1-800-542-2595 or fax 1-877-542-2596.

Cataloging-in-Publication Data

Names: Morlock, Theresa.
Title: Red-Tailed hawk vs. burmese python / Theresa Morlock.
Description: New York : Gareth Stevens Publishing, 2019. | Series: Bizarre beast battles | Includes glossary and index.
Identifiers: LCCN ISBN 9781538219379 (pbk.) | ISBN 9781538219355 (library bound) | ISBN 9781538219386 (6 pack)
Subjects: LCSH: Red-tailed hawk–Juvenile literature. | Burmese python–Juvenile literature.
Classification: LCC QL696.F32 M865 2019 | DDC 598.9'44–dc23

First Edition

Published in 2019 by
Gareth Stevens Publishing
111 East 14th Street, Suite 349
New York, NY 10003

Copyright © 2019 Gareth Stevens Publishing

Designer: Katelyn E. Reynolds
Editor: Monika Davies

Photo credits: Cover, p. 1 (red-tailed hawk) Ronnie Howard/Shutterstock.com; cover, p. 1 (Burmese python) Girish HC/Shutterstock.com; cover, pp. 1–24 (background texture) Apostrophe/Shutterstock.com; pp. 4–21 (hawk icon) denniro/Shutterstock.com; pp. 4–21 (python icon) Alfmaler/Shutterstock.com; p. 5 mlorenz/Shutterstock.com; pp. 7, 17 Heiko Kiera/Shutterstock.com; p. 8 Ondrej Prosicky/Shutterstock.com; p. 9 GOLFX/Shutterstock.com; p. 10 Tathoms/Shutterstock.com; p. 11 Sukpaiboonwat/Shutterstock.com; p. 12 studiolaska/Shutterstock.com; p. 13 LesPalenik/Shutterstock.com; p. 14 Ian Duffield/Shutterstock.com; pp. 15, 21 (burmese python) lunatic67/Shutterstock.com; p. 16 Svoboda Pavel/Shutterstock.com; p. 18 Jim Lambert/Shutterstock.com; p. 19 Vince Adam/Shutterstock.com p. 21 (red-tailed hawk) CampCrazy Photography/Shutterstock.com.

Printed in the United States of America

CPSIA compliance information: Batch #CS18GS: For further information contact Gareth Stevens, New York, New York at 1-800-542-2595.

CONTENTS

Words in the glossary appear in **bold** type the first time they are used in the text.

HAWKS HIGH ABOVE

Red-tailed hawks fly high in the sky. They fly in wide circles, searching for **prey** with their sharp eyes. They perch, or sit, in tall trees and on telephone poles looking for mice or rabbits below. These hawks have wide, rounded wings covered in dark brown feathers. Their undersides are cream-colored. Their tails are, of course, red!

Red-tailed hawks are the most common hawks in North America. They prefer to be out in the open and can often be seen in fields.

IN THE WILD, RED-TAILED HAWKS CAN LIVE FOR MORE THAN 20 YEARS.

5

SNAKES THAT SNEAK

Slithering snakes can be a scary sight! Burmese pythons are big, strong snakes. They have tan-colored skin with dark patterns along their back and sides. These snakes are carnivores, or meat eaters. They feed on birds and small animals. Larger Burmese pythons sometimes eat bigger prey, such as deer!

Burmese pythons are **native** to Southeast Asia where they live in the jungles and **marshes**. But, these massive snakes are now found all over the world. Many Burmese pythons have invaded the Florida Everglades—and they're taking over!

Young Burmese pythons spend a lot of their time in trees! But, as they grow, the pythons become too heavy to climb well.

7

WHICH IS BIGGER?

Picture a red-tailed hawk and a Burmese python sitting beside each other. If they faced off in a battle, which animal do you think would win?

 LENGTH:
18 TO 26 INCHES (45.7 TO 66 CM) LONG

 WEIGHT:
1.5 TO 3.2 POUNDS (0.7 TO 1.5 KG)

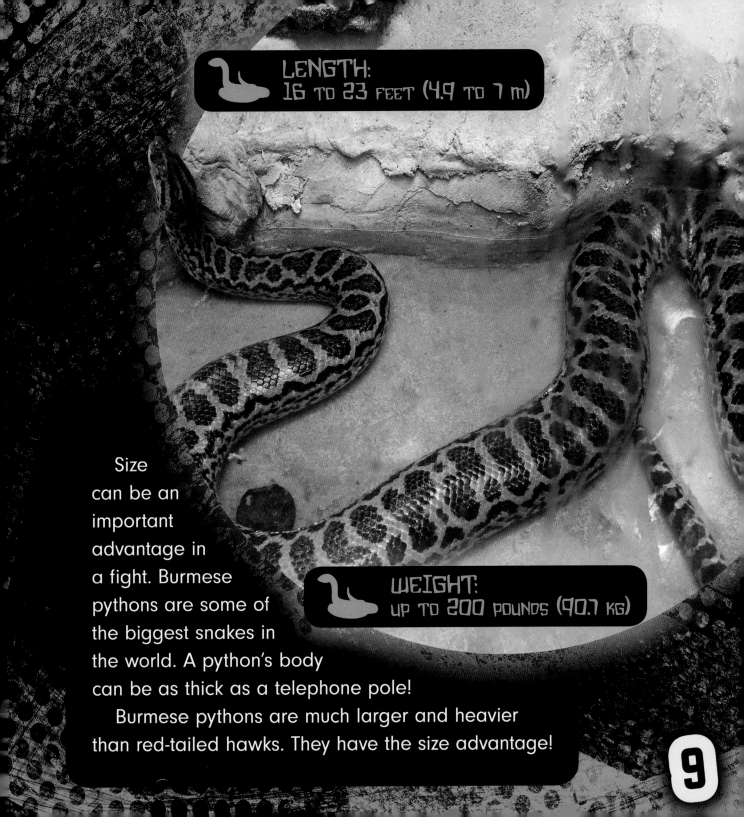

LENGTH:
16 TO 23 FEET (4.9 TO 7 m)

WEIGHT:
UP TO 200 POUNDS (90.7 KG)

Size can be an important advantage in a fight. Burmese pythons are some of the biggest snakes in the world. A python's body can be as thick as a telephone pole!

Burmese pythons are much larger and heavier than red-tailed hawks. They have the size advantage!

9

WHICH IS FASTER?

A red-tailed hawk might not be as big as a Burmese python, but is the bird faster than the snake? Red-tail hawks have wings that spread wide. Their broad, long wings help these hawks fly fast.

 AVERAGE SPEED OF A RED-TAILED HAWK: About 30 miles (48 km) per hour

 DIVING SPEED OF A RED-TAILED HAWK: About 120 miles (193 km) per hour

Burmese pythons may be big, but these snakes don't move very quickly. In fact, they usually act rather passive, or laid-back. However, they're strong swimmers and spend a lot of time in the water.

Although they're smaller, red-tailed hawks would win any race against Burmese pythons!

11

HUNTING HABITS

Red-tailed hawks are raptors, or birds of prey. They sometimes hunt in pairs, using teamwork to find and catch their food.

RED-TAILED HAWK'S HUNTING TOOLS:
* USES THEIR SHARP EYESIGHT TO HUNT
* CAN SEE A SPECIAL RANGE OF COLORS THAT HUMANS AREN'T ABLE TO SEE
* CAN SEE A MOUSE FROM 100 FEET (30 m) IN THE AIR

Pythons hunt their prey with their mouths! They flick, or quickly move, their tongues in and out to pick up scent **particles** in the air. These particles can carry the smell of the python's prey. The particles then go to a special **organ** in the top of the python's mouth. This is how pythons use their tongue to "smell" where their prey is hiding!

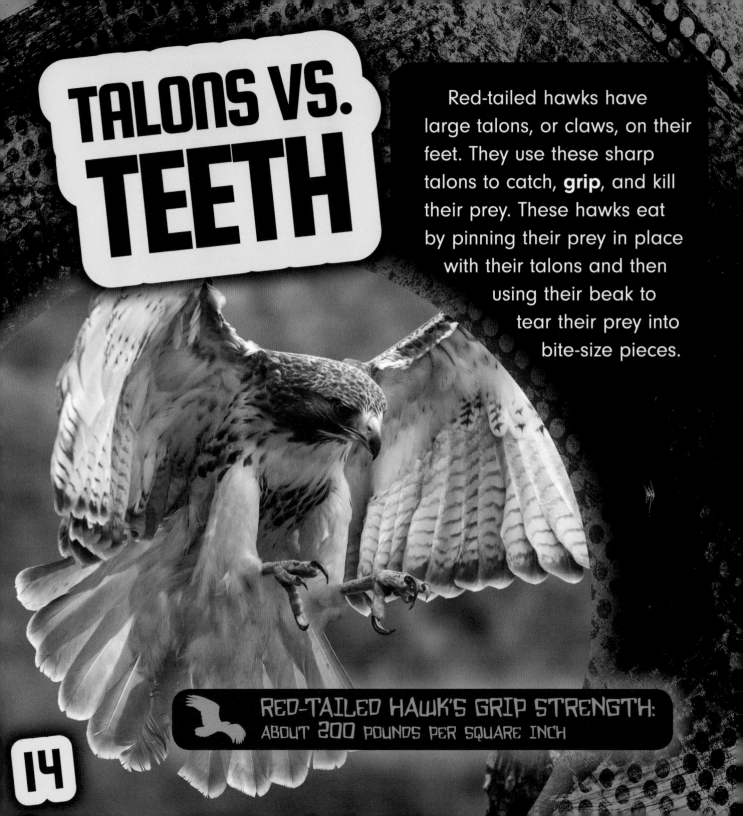

TALONS VS. TEETH

Red-tailed hawks have large talons, or claws, on their feet. They use these sharp talons to catch, **grip**, and kill their prey. These hawks eat by pinning their prey in place with their talons and then using their beak to tear their prey into bite-size pieces.

RED-TAILED HAWK'S GRIP STRENGTH:
ABOUT 200 POUNDS PER SQUARE INCH

Burmese pythons have teeth that curve backward so they can catch and hold their prey. These pythons then **coil** around their prey, gripping and **squeezing** it to death. Could the red-tailed hawk's sharp talons beat the Burmese python's deadly squeeze?

15

SPECIAL SKILLS

Red-tailed hawks are survivors. They're able to live in many different **habitats**. While these hawks like open spaces, they can also live in the mountains or rain forests.

RED-TAILED HAWK'S SUPER SKILLS:
* READY TO HUNT AT ANY TIME OF DAY
* CAN ADAPT, OR CHANGE, ITS HUNTING STYLE TO ATTACK DIFFERENT ANIMALS
* SOMETIMES WILL WAIT UNTIL ITS PREY ISN'T PAYING ATTENTION
* CAN ALSO **AMBUSH** ITS PREY FROM BEHIND A COVER OF TREES

Burmese pythons can swallow their meals whole. They have special **tissue** in their jaws that lets them open their mouth wide. This means they can swallow objects that are much larger than their mouth.

Compare the red-tailed hawk's skills with the Burmese python's skills. Which survival skills do you think are more helpful?

17

TOUGHEST ENEMIES

Red-tailed hawks usually live in the same territory their whole life. They hunt, nest, and care for their young within this area. Though they have few natural predators, they must compete for nest sites with great horned owls.

TOP ENEMIES OF THE RED-TAILED HAWK:

- HUMANS
- GREAT HORNED OWLS (PREDATORS OF HAWKS' EGGS AND BABY HAWKS)
- CROWS (PREDATORS OF HAWKS' EGGS AND BABY HAWKS)

TOP ENEMIES OF THE BURMESE PYTHON:
- HUMANS
- AMERICAN ALLIGATORS

Burmese pythons are top predators. They've even been known to eat alligators! In the Florida Everglades, Burmese pythons are an **invasive species**. There's a push to reduce the number of pythons in South Florida, so people are now allowed to hunt these snakes on state land.

19

FACE-OFF!

Imagine if a red-tailed hawk saw a Burmese python with its powerful eyesight. If the hawk flew down and attacked the snake, what do you think would happen? Would the hawk's speed be a match for the python's much larger size?

Or, would the python's special ability to sense prey with its tongue allow it to strike the hawk first? Do you think the squeeze of the hawk's talons would be enough to break the grip of the python?

In a face-off between these two deadly predators, there's no telling who would win!

It's unlikely red-tailed hawks and Burmese pythons would meet in the wild. Though both animals can be found in North America, they live in different habitats.

GLOSSARY

ambush: to attack from a hiding place

coil: to curl around and around

grip: to grab or hold something tightly

habitat: the natural place where an animal or plant lives

invasive species: one kind of living thing likely to spread and be harmful when placed in a new area

jaws: the bones that hold the teeth and make up the mouth

marsh: an area of soft, wet land

native: existing naturally in a certain area

organ: a part inside an animal's body

particle: a very small piece of something

prey: an animal that is hunted by other animals for food

squeeze: to press something tightly

tissue: matter that forms the parts of living things

FOR MORE INFORMATION

BOOKS

Aronin, Miriam. *Florida's Burmese Pythons: Squeezing the Everglades*. New York, NY: Bearport Publishing, 2016.

Hill, Melissa. *Red-Tailed Hawks*. Mankato, MN: Capstone Press, 2015.

Oachs, Emily Rose. *Burmese Pythons*. Minneapolis, MN: Bellwether Media, 2014.

WEBSITES

Red-Tailed Hawk
biokids.umich.edu/critters/Buteo_jamaicensis/
Learn more interesting facts about red-tailed hawks here.

Giant Snake of the Everglades—The Invasive Burmese Python
discoverykids.com/tvshow/giant-snake-of-the-everglades-the-invasive-burmese-python/
Watch this video to get up close and personal with a Burmese python in the Florida Everglades!

INDEX